GOLF INSTRUCTOR'S LIBRARY

OFF THE TEE

MICHAEL HOBBS

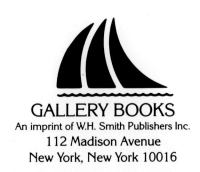

GALLERY BOOKS
An imprint of W.H. Smith Publishers Inc.
112 Madison Avenue
New York, New York 10016

A QUINTET BOOK

Produced for GALLERY BOOKS
An imprint of W. H. Smith Publishers Inc.
112 Madison Avenue
New York, New York 10016

ISBN 0–8317–3871–5

This book was designed and produced by
Quintet Publishing Limited
6 Blundell Street
London N7 9BH

Creative Director: Terry Jeavons
Art Director: Ian Hunt
Project Editor: David Barraclough
Illustrator: Rob Shone
Photographer: Michael Hobbs

Typeset in Great Britain by
Central Southern Typesetters, Eastbourne
Manufactured in Hong Kong by
Regent Publishing Services Limited
Printed in Hong Kong by
Leefung-Asco Printers Limited

**Although the PGA now officially uses the term 'the
hold', throughout this book refers to 'the grip', which is
still commonly used among golfers.**

CONTENTS

PREFACE

I am a left-handed golfer. However, over the years I haven't found it difficult to follow golf instruction writing, which is traditionally directed at right-handers.

As a golf writer, I know that always mentioning each form of the golfing species is easily possible, but leads to many repetitive phrases that impair the readability of the book. As a left-hander I know we have learned to cope in a 90 per cent right-handed world. A right-hander, on the other hand, is far less able. I don't think he could follow a text written for left-handers – imagine him trying to use left-handed scissors or knock in a tack, grasping the hammer left-handed. What injuries and incompetence would result for this less adaptable and accomplished sector of the human species!

ACKNOWLEDGEMENTS

Above all, I should like to thank Grenville Warne for being a splendid model for my instructional photography. He gave up many hours throughout a whole season when he would surely far rather have been playing than demonstrating. His help has been invaluable.

I should like to thank my main golf club, Tracy Park near Bristol, England, for allowing me to carry out most of the instruction photography on its splendid 27 holes. I also thank other clubs for more limited photographic facilities.

The club's professional, Grant Aitken, and his son and assistant professional Kelvin, have also been invariably helpful with advice, information and allowing me to use equipment for illustrations.

At Quintet Publishing, I should particularly like to thank David Barraclough for his continuous work throughout the project and also Peter Arnold who was responsible for the detailed copy editing. My thanks are also due to Rob Shone for his production of drawings and diagrams and the design team at Bridgewater Design.

Michael Hobbs   Worcester, England

HOLDING THE CLUB FOR FULL SHOTS

Even champions have used unconventional, and for that matter, downright bad grips. One can remember Gene Sarazen in the past, and Lee Trevino, now a dominant force on the US Seniors Tour. Among today's top tournament professionals, the same could be said for Paul Azinger and Bernhard Langer, and among the ladies, there's Nancy Lopez, all of whom place their left hands in a position which many would consider wrong.

They're all outstanding golfers, so one is entitled to ask if they're right and the rest of the golfing world at fault. The answer is that, if you are to use an unconventional grip, then compensations must be made elsewhere in the swing. A relatively poor player may well find that this doesn't work at all, while a more talented golfer will experience periods of poor play.

So there are very good arguments for using a conventional grip. We now need to define just what that is. It might be useful if you have a club to hand while we're doing this.

The first thing to remember is that the club is held mainly in the fingers – and small variations will apply depending on whether you have long and lean, or more spatulate ones. Start with the idea that the basic grip is palm-to-palm, with the handle of the club in between. Now let's take one hand at a time, first noting where the club lies across the open hand.

The handle should run from the bottom joint of the little finger of the left hand to the first joint of the forefinger, and you'll note that the palm is a definite help at the little finger end. The right-hand grip lies just a little more in the fingers themselves, perhaps by no more than a quarter of an inch.

Ready to play.

How the club lies across the left hand.

Left hand closed.

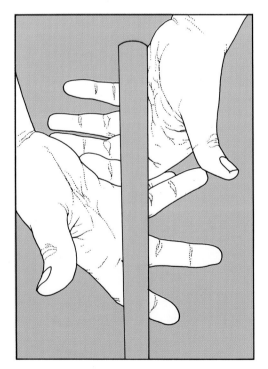

How the club lies across the open hands.

Now, allow your hand to close naturally, and note the position of your thumbs. You'll find that they lie almost straight down the shaft, with the left thumb offset a little to the right, and the right thumb to the left. Looking down from your stance position, you should see only the first two knuckles of your left hand.

This is the basic, conventional grip; all fingers on the shaft, with the hands nestling close together. However, because the hands tend to work better in unison if they are more definitely linked, this grip is seldom taught today.

THE 'VARDON' GRIP

Early golf clubs featured much thicker grips than today's implements. This meant that most good players nestled the club much more firmly in the palms than you'll see around the circuits today: neither thumb rested on the shaft.

Over the years, shafts became thinner and, round about 1890, a few people began to use a new way of melding the hands together. The right hand moved a little way up the shaft with the little finger no longer gripping it. Instead, it came to rest over the left forefinger, or perhaps a little further up, in the gap between the first two fingers.

How the club lies across the right hand.

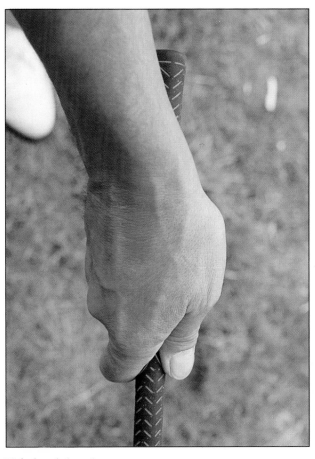

Right hand closed.

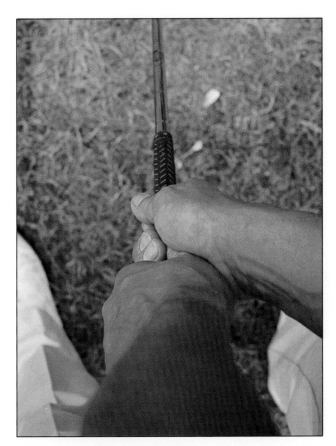

Player's view of the completed grip.

The double overlapping grip – a variation on the Vardon grip.

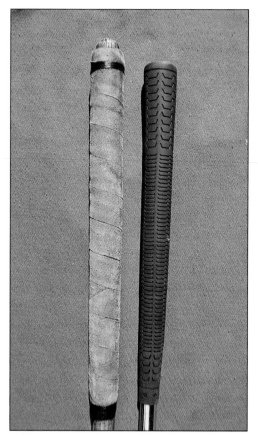

A thicker sheepskin grip of the past and a modern rubber grip.

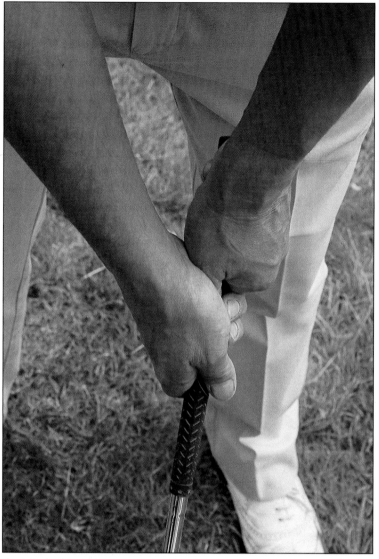

The interlocking grip.

The rest of the golfing world was slow to follow suit, because most of the best players carried on in the same old way. However, from the mid-1890's, the 'Great Triumvirate' of J H Taylor, Harry Vardon and James Braid all adopted the 'overlap' grip, and people began to sit up and take notice. Obviously, if the 'Great Triumvirate' did it, it must be right.

Quite naturally, special attention was paid to Harry Vardon, who between 1896 and 1900 played a quality of golf that had never been seen before. Not only that, but he *looked* the perfect golfer as well, and his grip was much imitated. Eventually it became called the 'Vardon Grip'. Not that he, in fact, invented it, or was particularly unusual in using it.

THE INTERLOCKING GRIP

This, again, is simply a way to link the hands together. Here, the left forefinger isn't on the shaft at all. It rests in the gap

The Great Triumvirate – Taylor, Braid and Vardon – by Clement Flower, 1913.

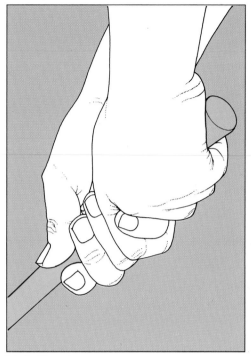

Interlocking grip.

A double overlapping grip on the green.

between the last two fingers of the right hand, with the right little finger placed between forefinger and middle finger of the left hand.

If you use this grip, you'll notice that only three fingers of each hand (plus the thumbs, as before), rest on the club shaft. For many, this grip doesn't feel comfortable, but it is an effective way of locking the hands together. Most professionals prefer the Vardon Grip, but Jack Nicklaus and Greg Norman use the interlock, so it must have much to recommend it.

VARIATIONS

Just as the ten-fingered grip is out of favour, quite a few excellent players have adopted more overlap than is the norm. It's quite possible to overlap two fingers, and some players have even extended this to three, which leaves only the forefinger on the actual grip of the club. Usually, this is

Where the Vs should point.

Hands turned counter-clockwise.

The Vs have dropped below the right shoulder.

done by players who want to minimize the domination of their right hands, often to avoid hooking.

CHECKING ON WHERE THE 'V's POINT

The gaps between forefinger and thumb of both right and left hands form a 'V' shape when the hands close around the club. When you view this from your stance, or in a mirror, the apex of both V's should point approximately towards your right shoulder.

There are variations, however. Professionals with particularly strong and lively hands have often turned both of them a little anti-clockwise. Those V's will then point somewhere between the chin and the point of the right shoulder, depending on what they feel works best for them. But please note – no one goes in the other direction, so that the V's drop to below the right shoulder.

RULES AND GOLF COURSE BEHAVIOUR

Far too many golfers, when they first take up the game, get their priorities wrong.

First, probably, comes the appealing glitter and sheen of a brand new set of clubs. It might be closely followed by colour coordinated clothing, with matching umbrella and golfbag. Amazingly, this often happens before the golfer has taken a single lesson, even before he or she has tried hitting a single golf ball. Remember, though most have sufficient innate ability to become reasonable players eventually, there is, alas, a small minority who don't.

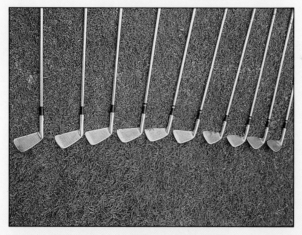

A full set of irons clearly showing the varying degrees of loft.

Before going to all this expense, I advise you go to a practice range and, perhaps even more important, have a few lessons. This will ensure you start correctly as regards, for example, the right grip and stance. Some things, these in particular, are very hard to change once they become ingrained.

Even if you pass these hurdles successfully, you are still not ready to step on to a golf course.

Why? Well, have you thought of acquainting yourself with the rules of golf and behaviour on the course? The rules are lengthy and sometimes difficult to understand. They have to be complicated because the game is played cross country. You can find yourself in situations that could not possibly occur in the strictly defined areas used in tennis, football and squash, for example. There is probably no other game that is so complex as regards the rules, and all as a result of the terrain over which the game is played.

It isn't the aim of *The Golf Instructor's Library* to set out all the rules of golf. That would take a book in itself to both explain the rules and give examples of their application. However, all is by no means lost. Books are already available on the subject and both the Royal and Ancient Golf Club of St Andrews and the United States Golf Association provide rule books of a size which can be kept permanently in your golf bag.

Golf course behaviour is a little different. You will easily find short passages on 'etiquette', but these don't go into sufficient detail. Even if you attempt to study the subject, there will still be gaps in your knowledge which can only be filled by watching how experienced players conduct themselves during a round of golf.

But what is at the root of 'etiquette'? The word makes it sound rather like a Victorian manual aimed at teaching people how to handle the cutlery at upper class dinner parties or how to address the wife of the president of the United States or the consort of the Queen of England!

Golfing 'etiquette' is how you behave towards both your fellow golfers and the golf course.

For this book I'll confine myself to how you behave on the tee as a player in the most common form of golf, a fourball.

Firstly, it is obviously quite important to avoid killing or maiming your companions! Be very careful about those loosening up practice swings. Drift a reasonable distance away from your fellow players. A golf club is a lethal weapon. A clubhead travelling at around 100 mph can crack a skull, blind a person and break all manner of bones. Make sure no one is anywhere near where you are swinging your club and remember that your fellow players may easily wander into the path of your swing.

Also remember that – even if only occasionally – clubheads have been known to fly off. Make the aim of your swing, therefore, in the opposite direction to where your fellow golfers are standing.

Quite often in those swings, you'll be taking divots. Your fellow players will not wish to be hit by flying turf. You may feel that this is unlikely to do much bodily harm, but being hit in the face, or simply having divots flying close by, can be quite a shock. And you could dislodge a stone along with the turf divot and remove someone's eye. Once more, then, direct your swing away from other golfers.

The next danger to other players comes when you stand on the tee and play your shot. You are unlikely to be wild enough to strike a member of your fourball this time, but beware of others on the golf course. Are you quite sure that the players in the match immediately ahead of you are out of range? Imagine that you are going to hit the longest drive of your life. If you are confident that you won't reach anyone playing ahead, play your shot, but bear in mind that we only know our length limits on very familiar courses. Very few have good enough judgement to know that, say, 270 yards is the distance to the third oak tree along the right-hand side of the fairway Caution is therefore the watch word and you'll only need to wait a few seconds for those ahead to walk the extra yards.

These players are not out of range.

There are other players on the course and you need to glance around. Perhaps there's a tee with a group of players standing on it within range. A glance at your scorecard, or even a notice on your own tee, may tell you that you are not permitted to drive off when that other tee is occupied.

Golf courses also frequently have parallel fairways. Is there someone ahead who has come into your line of fire in order to play their ball? If so, you have 'right of way' but you may feel guilty if your ball strikes this player.

There may be other players within range but, because most golf courses are busy, no one can be expected to wait until there is no possibility of your ball hitting players should you happen to be very wild.

However, there's still something you are required to do in these circumstances. Be ready to give a full-throated cry of 'Fore!'

But perhaps you shouldn't be on the tee at all. Is it actually your turn to play? If you are a beginner, or a stranger at the particular golf club, follow their procedures. In a strokeplay competition, for instance, it's usual for the order on the draw sheet to be followed. In fourball play, it may be the club tradition that the golfer with the lowest handicap is the first to tee off. Most often it is done 'by lot' – in other words the toss of a coin. In all this, there isn't really a problem. Just have the courtesy to ask or wait until others tell you.

The players watching this tee shot are in correct positions.

Now let's turn to the behaviour expected of you when another member of your game is on the tee. It's quite simple and mainly concerns where you stand and what not to do. You shouldn't stand behind the player's line of shot since many object to this, nor should you stand too far in front. Both these positions can catch your fellow golfer's eye and are distracting. Similarly you should not be behind the player's back. Golfers about to hit the ball are very often nervy fellows. They like to know where you are. Therefore, you stand, not too close, facing their chest and, of course, clear of the teeing ground.

Well, we've now got you in the right place. You are still in a position where any movement could catch his or her eye. So stand still and don't make any noise. You shouldn't, for example, be talking to other players, causing coins to chink in your pocket or moving your golf bag.

As with all rules of golf or golf behaviour, there are exceptions. When the light is dim towards dusk,

The player on the right is too far behind the driver.

or if a low sun is shining into a player's eyes, it is difficult to follow the flight of the ball. In such cases, it's certainly permissible to stand behind the player's line of shot. You are far more likely to be able to track the ball from that position rather than side on. But ask first.

It's also a courtesy to follow the flight of your fellow players' golf balls. You hope they'll do the same for you. It also saves time. The striker, even in the clearest of light, may fail to catch sight of their ball, usually if it's flown high or to right or left.

Also make a mental note of where other golf balls finish. It can prevent a long search and, of course, a lost ball that would have easily been found if, in this case, four golfers were looking in the right area.

Nowadays much time is devoted to golf on television. Usually this shows golfers playing for their livelihood and often large amounts of money. One result is many tournament players take the game at a very slow pace. They debate their choice of club, select one and then have a change of mind. Quite often more than once. When the decision is eventually made, a few practice swings may follow and the golfer takes some time examining their target line from behind the ball. Then a stance is taken up and a few, or perhaps a large number of waggles follow. All that done, and there may still be a pause before taking the momentous decision to begin the backswing.

Keep in mind how relatively quickly golf used to be played before we began to imitate the stars. Indeed, the stars of bygone days also played at a fast pace. The golfer used to walk quickly, make up their mind on choice of club and how to play it before reaching their ball, and then took up their stance briskly and swung. Two hours for a two ball to play 18 holes was the norm, and not so very much more for four players.

Alas, that's not remotely possible today, except when you have the luck to find an empty course ahead of you. If you are a paragon of briskness, you will still be held up by the players in your own game and blocked by the games ahead of you.

The best you can aim for is not to be the cause of slow play. Always bear in mind how golfers of the past approached the game.

All this has to do with behaviour, rather than that word 'etiquette' in its old-fashioned sense. However, the word does come into the modern game of golf as regards clothing.

It is correct to stand behind a player when the light is dim.

Time to consider packing up and returning to the clubhouse. Playing in the dark can be dangerous.

The part of the teeing area you are concerned with is a rectangle. It is the area defined by an imaginary straight line drawn between the tee markers you are playing from that day, extending towards the rear of the teeing ground for two club (driver) lengths, with a second parallel line drawn across to complete the rectangle. You must not place your ball any nearer to the hole than the front line, or anywhere else outside the dimensions of the rectangle. If you do, you are penalized two strokes in strokeplay (and disqualified if you don't replay the shot) and can be required to replay the tee shot in matchplay. Most opponents will only

Many golfers like to get themselves up in resplendent garb. If you are one, I have no objections. I'll simply concentrate on a few of the 'don'ts'.

Dress rules at golf clubs vary and have a broad range. At your own club, you simply have to learn them and conform. If they are, some might say, too lax, this won't necessarily be the case elsewhere.

You are never wrong, however, kitted out in a pair of golf shoes, slacks, a shirt with a collar and a plain sweater. That's simple enough. However, if you turn out in, for example, trainers, shorts or jeans, a tee shirt and a jockey cap you could easily not be allowed on the course.

The point to bear in mind is that, all over the world, clubs and public courses are not at all strict about golf clothing – but there are restrictions from time to time and it's easy to avoid offending.

So much for behaviour. Though the rules of golf are generally complex, they aren't as regards tee shots since you are on the only part of a golf course that is defined as exactly as the dimensions of, for example, a tennis court.

This ball is clearly not in front of the tee marker.

TOP AND ABOVE: Look for a good flat tie on the tee, rather than tee up as far as possible.

ask you to do this if you hit a particularly good shot. The penalty is far less severe than in strokeplay, but certainly irritating if you've just dispatched a screamer of a drive or holed in one at a par 3.

A surprising number of people do tee their ball up just an inch or two further forward than the rules allow, even though the advantage is virtually non-existant. Is a drive of 260 yards 3 inches really any better than one of 260 yards. The extra distance might mean your ball just reaches a bunker or divot hole. Remember, your fellow golfers in matchplay will seldom require you to replay the shot. But they will almost always notice and put you down in their memories as a cheat. In strokeplay, they are required to take action.

However, there is no reason why you shouldn't take maximum advantage of the rectangle. Examine it for a flat lie or perhaps just the merest suggestion of an upslope, if that's what you prefer. Be prepared to lose a little distance to get this. Also make sure that you have chosen ground which provides a good stance, so that you won't, for instance, have a foot on a loose divot.

In order to hit away from trouble along the left, tee up on the extreme left of the tee.

Incidentally, only the ball has to be within the teeing rectangle – you don't. Though it is rarely an advantage to stand outside, there are occasions when it can be. These are frequently ignored by the vast majority of golfers. Let's suppose there's a frightening hazard all along the left of the fairway ahead. You want to aim away from it. The further left you stand, the better. So why not take full advantage of the rules and stand outside the teeing area?

Having now made all the decisions, you are ready to play your shot and the ball falls off the tee peg. You can simply replace it, without penalty. But this time be sure it's secure on its perch. If it falls off as your clubhead approaches the ball, even a reasonable shot is unlikely and the stroke counts if you are in the process of making it.

Now, you've hit your ball away and, alas, it's heading for wild country where you are not confident that you can find the ball. After the remaining players have teed off, you have the option of playing another shot. But first you have a decision to make. You can declare the ball lost, in which case it's officially abandoned. You can't play it even if it is later found. You have penalized yourself one stroke and distance, and your second tee shot counts as your third.

Often, however, golfers simply don't know whether or not they are going to find a ball. In this case, tell your fellow golfers that you are playing a 'provisional ball'. There is nothing in the rules to prevent your doing so after every shot and you certainly should whenever you are unsure whether your ball will be found.

In this instance, if your first tee shot is found, you must play that ball. Should it be in an unplayable lie, you should follow the rules for that situation (dealt with in *Trouble Shooting*).

Playing one (even two) provisional balls is often sensible. If your first shot is lost, it avoids the delay of having to walk back to the tee.

Just as there are simple dress pointers to follow before you play off the first tee, so you must be equipped as the rules of golf require. Remember to check that you have no more than 14 clubs in your bag. If you find an extra one, you don't have to dispose of it. You can nominate to your fellow players which club is out of play.

Each club must also conform to the rules of the game, but there should be no problem with manufactured clubs. Should you happen to make yourself a club, however, look up the rules regarding what constitutes an illegal piece of equipment.

As regards your ball, you should make sure you can identify it. Strictly speaking, just to know you are playing, say, a number 4 Titleist isn't quite good enough. For a start, declare the make and number of your ball to your fellow players to avoid any confusion. To make doubly sure, put an identifying mark on your ball.

STANDING AND SWINGING

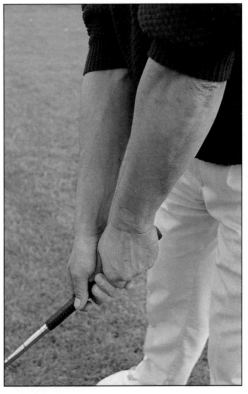

A tight Vardon grip.

Professionals, who play and practise every day, develop extremely strong hands. It doesn't take them any special effort to hold the club very firmly indeed when playing a full swing. In contrast, club golfers play very much less, often averaging, say, one game per weekend, so obviously, their fingers don't have the opportunity to become nearly as strong as those of a professional.

Nevertheless, it's important to avoid gripping the club tightly, forcing the muscles of forearm, upper arm and shoulders to become taut.

Unfortunately, it *feels* necessary to grip tightly, because everyone is aware how important the hands are: they are, after all, the only connection between the club and you. The answer is to concentrate on being firm, not tight. It's impossible to swing back and through freely with a tight grip, and it's all too easy to lose vital clubhead speed.

Keep supple on the backswing. Your grip will firm up quite naturally when in the hitting area.

Reaching for the ball.

A cramped stance.

FINDING YOUR NATURAL BALL POSITION

Many poor golfers stand with the ball too far away, and therefore find themselves leaning over much too far when attempting to make a full shot. Far fewer people stand too close to the ball, inhibiting their ability to swing freely. Somewhere between these two extremes there's a right position for you. Here's how to find it.

Stand with your feet apart, at about shoulder width. Stand erect, with knees flexed, bottom slightly out, and let your arms support the club, not allowing it to dangle. Now, without bending your back, lean down from the waist. The spot where the clubhead touches the ground is where your ball should be.

Feet at shoulder width.

Now bend from the waist.

And you're in the right position.

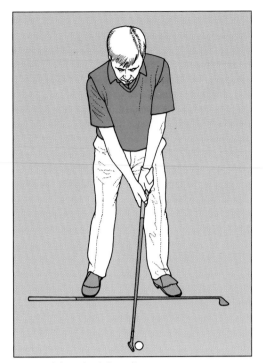

Using a club to check feet alignment.

ABOVE AND OPPOSITE: This par 4 is occasionally driveable – wind behind, running fairway – but usually it would be better to play an accurate iron shot. There's a tree in play close by on the left, bunkers beyond, and on the right, more trees.

THE FEET

Observe your feet when you're walking normally. Henry Cotton is slightly pigeon toed, and stood to the ball that way. Most of us, however, splay our toes outward to some degree, and you should do the same when standing to the ball.

A line drawn across your toes should be exactly parallel with a line from your ball to the target.

At some point, you might like to experiment with your left foot drawn back, just a little, but begin from the normal position – and remember, shoulders and hips must also be parallel with the target line.

Visualizing the line to the target.

AIM THE CLUBFACE

Far too many golfers think of settling into position over the ball. There is, then, much shuffling of feet to line up for the shot, and concentration on having the ball a comfortable distance away. Only after that do they look up to see where the target is.

Wrong!

There's a much better way of going about things. As you walk up to the ball, visualize a line from it to the target. When you arrive, first aim your club face along that target line. It's up to you how you do it.

Most golfers used to do this with just the left hand on the club, and then add the other hand once they were satisfied that the clubface was on line. Today, right-hand-first is more popular.

Aligning the left hand first.

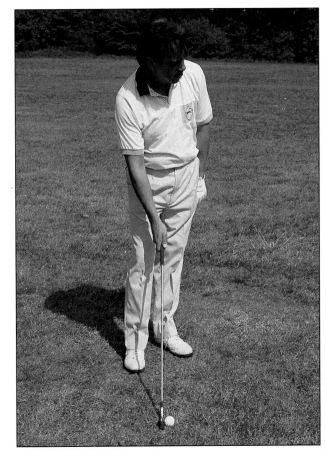

Aligning right hand first.

ABOVE LEFT AND RIGHT: The player is reaching round, not under, to get his right hand in position.

ABOVE LEFT AND RIGHT: Here, he reaches under. Note how the right shoulder is lower than the left now.

This does give one very clear advantage. Many poor players tend to reach *round* to place the right hand in position when the left hand is placed on the club first. But, if you are going to keep your shoulders square with the target line, you must reach *under* with your right hand. Reaching round throws the shoulders, and very possibly the hips as well, wide open. A slice or pull hook is the virtually certain result.

Once you have your hands on the club, and the face is aimed, let the rest of your body join in. This means aligning the shoulder and hips along the target line, getting the distance between you and the ball right, and allowing the knees to flex slightly.

This is the orthodox square position. After much experiment, however, many good players have found that it suits them better to stand in a slightly open position, left foot withdrawn from the line by an inch or two. They maintain that this helps them not to hook the ball, and that it allows them to swing through more freely because the left hip is not so much 'in the way'.

But the converse isn't true. If you are a slicer, you won't find a cure by moving your left foot a little closer to the ball. For most people, the increased difficulty of swinging freely through and clearing your hips will make cutting across the ball more likely.

Some like to set the right foot in position first.

Seve Ballesteros demonstrates his driving technique.

SWINGING BACK

The most important part of the backswing is unarguably the very first movement, simply because it influences everything that follows. Those first two or three inches can make or destroy a swing.

Some players need a trigger to start the whole thing off, a movement of some kind *towards* the ball. This is just an aid to starting the take-away, so there's nothing rigid about it; it can be made with knees, hands or legs and is almost imperceptible.

Many players also find a preliminary 'waggle' is useful. This is a rehearsal, in miniature, of the whole swing. The golfer moves the clubhead a foot or two away from the ball, then brings it back to what will be the point of impact.

This shouldn't be a vague waving of the club to and fro. The idea isn't merely to loosen the muscles and relax the nerves, but rather to programme the muscles for the task ahead.

The 'waggle' will differ from shot to shot. It will be very different for a full drive than for a little high lob shot over a bunker with the green close behind. In the first case you will be rehearsing power; in the second, a delicate touch.

Some players take a rather different view of the 'waggle' They are interested in just the very beginning of the take-away, the part which gets the whole swing going rhythmically and in line. They are reassuring themselves and programming the muscle memory for the beginning of the take-away.

Yet many play with no apparent movements of any kind, once they have settled into the stance. My own opinion is that there are, in fact, such movements but they are internal and imperceptible. The golfer is, perhaps, feeling his or her balance and making minute changes to weight distribution – a little, more or less, towards the heels. Often that motionless period can be quite brief, in the case of a player like Seve Ballesteros. It may be the result of the player waiting until he or she 'feels ready'.

This waggle rehearses the beginning of the swing to come.

The first few inches of the backswing.

ABOVE AND RIGHT: Here the right leg is twisting and the foot rolling too much.

IT'S A ONE-PIECE MOVEMENT

Hands and arms should begin to move away from the ball, and shoulders turn, as a single, integrated movement. If you allow the hands to take over right away, as feels natural, they will dominate all through, and ruin your swing.

Very soon, your hips begin to follow the turning movements of your shoulders. Continue your turn with the ultimate aim of presenting your back to your target; your hips won't turn as much, finishing at about 45 degrees.

Now I'm not suggesting that you equip yourself with a protractor and measure off 45 degrees. Things are actually simpler than that. This is because the turn is made around the axle that is your right leg. Though it isn't rigid, and remains flexed, as in your stance position, it must not move, or that sweet swing of yours will become a sway, and you may well find yourself hopelessly off balance.

If you maintain the position of your right leg, then that 45 degree angle of your hips follows automatically. They will simply not be able to move any further.

ABOVE AND BELOW: Stages of the backswing.

ABOVE AND RIGHT: A good leg position at the
top of the backswing.

WHAT HAPPENS TO THE WRISTS?

Your wrists have to flex at some point in your backswing. This can happen either naturally, or as a deliberate movement, in three different ways. They are:

(1) Flexing can be delayed until the end of the backswing, the last real movement in fact. There is one very clear advantage in this, in that the player is encouraged to make a full shoulder turn, and can keep that in mind as the main backswing thought. Only when the full shoulder turn has been made are the wrists allowed to break.

(2) This, somewhat confusingly, is the exact reverse of (1). The wrist-break is completed early, once the one-piece beginning of the backswing is accomplished.

This method, apparently, does nothing to help the golfer make the full shoulder turn, but it gets the wrist-break out of the way early, and is easier to perform at this point when the swing is still slow. If left to the last moment, the argument goes, the wrist-break can become involved in the transition from backswing to downswing.

(3) Flexing can be continuous and gradual, carried out right throughout the backswing. This is, perhaps, the most natural method, but it doesn't give the golfer any key swing thoughts to hang on to.

Early wrist break – sometimes called 'setting the angle early'.

Too much lift of the left heel.

This stance is better.

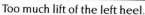

THE FEET

Although you are very likely to have spikes in the soles of your shoes, you certainly shouldn't be rooted to the ground by them. The pull exerted by your backswing will cause both feet to roll naturally, and it's quite likely that the left side and heel of your left foot will leave the ground. This is fine, and helps to give freedom to the swing, but your heel shouldn't be allowed to leave the ground completely. If it does, then you are lifting away from the ball, and not swinging.

Your right foot will roll very much less, as a result of the transfer of weight from the inside to the outside of the foot.

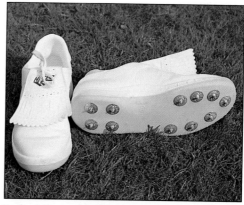

Spiked shoes should not prevent your feet from rolling during the backswing.

33

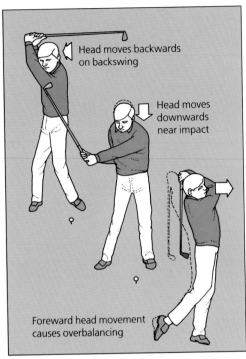

Head moves backwards on backswing

Head moves downwards near impact

Foreward head movement causes overbalancing

Keeping the head still during the swing is one of the novice's biggest problems. The above are the three most common head movement faults.

THE HEAD

No golfer can execute a full swing without moving the head. Many golfers have *thought* that they could, and although it's impossible, it's certainly something to aim at.

Good players do move their heads, but it's a relatively small movement which takes place in two directions. Perhaps the head moves a couple of inches backwards, increasing by an inch or more by impact, and a couple of inches downwards by the time the club strikes the ball. Even so, teachers tell their pupils not to move their heads and may, for example, place a hand on the head to check the amount of movement.

In an ideal world, the head would remain completely steady, but in practical terms, the turning of the shoulders creates a pull on the neck which is transferred into a head movement. Perhaps a robot could do it, but the human frame just isn't flexible enough.

So we must learn to live with it.

To start with the obvious, golf becomes a much more difficult game if your head turns so much that you can't see the ball when you are at the top of your backswing. Demands on a golfer's hand and eye co-ordination are quite severe enough without adding any more.

If you find that this is happening, then you must shorten the length of your backswing. The point at which the pull on neck muscles becomes extreme depends entirely on the body doing the swinging. While some people have to stop short, others can swing back well beyond the horizontal without untoward problems.

One thing you can do is to turn your head a little to the right in your initial set-up. Jack Nicklaus, in fact, makes a very definite turn of his head to the right, just before swinging back. He's got that head turn out of the way before the stroke commences.

Please – don't be too dispirited about my comments regarding unavoidable head movement. A blind man can play very good golf, providing he begins with clubhead to ball. In the same way, our memories do enable us to find the ball, even with the eyes shut.

Indeed, there have been very great golfers who played with far too much head movement. It used to be said of the great Walter Hagen, for example, that he 'began with a sway and ended with a lunge'. Among modern champions, Curtis Strange is renowned for the amount of sway in his swing.

So far, we have been considering the effects of lateral head movement. But your head can move up and down, as well as from side to side. Your head shouldn't be lifted by your arms and shoulder movement. If it is, you're not *turning* at the top of your backswing, but simply *lifting* your arms up.

Lifting the arms.

The Nicklaus head position before swinging.

In fact, you're not getting a swing at all. It's wise to check on this, either in a mirror, or by asking an onlooker.

On the other hand, your head may move forward as you come into the ball, which probably means you are throwing your body at the ball rather than the clubhead. Most good players involuntarily lower their heads a little in the impact zone, and their heads also move backwards. If they didn't, the golfer would lose balance and fall over!

A full backswing.

Fred Couples at the 1989 Ryder Cup.

SWING PLANES

Now we must visualize your swing plane. To do this, imagine a straight line, drawn from the base of your neck to the ball when you have taken up your stance. Alternatively, you could think of a large wheel in that same plane, with the base of your neck as the hub. The rim of that wheel would pass through the ball and extend to the same distance in the opposite direction.

As you stand to the ball, everything – clubhead, hands, arms, are inside the wheel. And should stay there, on backswing, downswing and through swing.

Let's look at some errors which send the swing outside that imaginary wheel, and see what results.

(1) At the very beginning of the take-away, the club can swing away from the body. Lee Trevino does this, as do many others. While there is little direct harm in this, it does add the complication of having to bring the club back on track.

(2) The arms may lift much later in the backswing, when the hands are at about shoulder level. In this case, the player is either not turning their shoulders properly, or simply doesn't have enough flexibility to swing properly.

However, the player has to get that clubhead well back, so the only thing to do is to *lift* it there.

It's just about impossible to recover from this position, and the clubhead is now outside your imaginary wheel. Admittedly, Miller Barber and James Bruen managed to avert disaster by looping the clubhead back inside the wheel, and did it very well, too, but for the average golfer it makes consistent play almost impossible.

If you don't loop back inside the wheel, what happens? Probably one of three things.

The ball may curve rapidly to the right, because you have cut across it from right to left, with the clubface more or less square-on to the ball.

On the other hand, the ball may go left, because while your swing path was satisfactory enough, you have hit it with the face more or less closed. In extreme cases, you can even endanger your left foot!

It could fly absolutely straight, in which case you have performed a bit of magic. You have cut across the ball from right to left, with your clubhead slightly closed. A classic case of two wrongs making a right. Even so, you'll lose distance, because the clubhead momentum isn't flowing straight down the target line.

All things considered, you'll agree that it must be simpler to deliver the clubhead to the ball along the right path; the deviations caused by the clubface not arriving square to the target line cause enough problems, anyway.

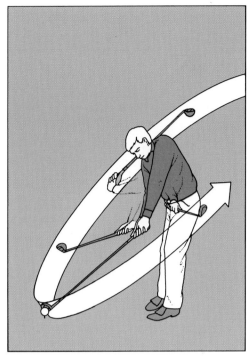

Arc of the clubhead during the swing.

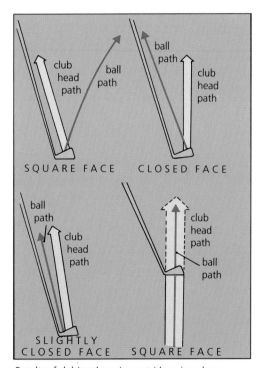

Results of clubhead moving outside swing plane.

This swing is too flat and is likely to create a pull or hook shot.

This swing is too upright and is likely to create the dreaded slice.

FLAT AND UPRIGHT SWING PLANES

If people criticize your swing as being either 'too upright' or 'too flat', you can probably ignore them. Ben Hogan and Jack Nicklaus would be in most people's list of the best six golfers ever, yet Hogan had a flat swing, and Nicklaus is upright. But both kept inside that imaginary wheel.

There are, however, extremes which must be avoided. If you're flat, don't let your plane get below shoulder level, and if upright, it's as well to avoid letting your backswing hit you on the head.

It seems to me that Nicklaus now swings on a considerably flatter plane than he used to – and will probably suffer less back trouble. On the other hand, Nicklaus's upright swing was hugely influential, simply because anything done by the world's best golfer is widely imitated. Consider the Vardon grip, in its day, or the sight of Bobby Jones playing his full shots with his feet close together.

It isn't wise, however, to imitate the great players too slavishly. While Vardon's grip was obviously impeccable,

ABOVE LEFT AND RIGHT: Average plane, different viewpoints.

Jones's stance would simply demand too much from the average golfer's balancing abilities. Similarly, the Hogan and Nicklaus swing planes, flat and upright respectively, are extremes, and unlikely to suit most golfers.

In 1990, Nick Faldo established himself, for a while anyway, as the world's greatest golfer. In spite of the fact that he stands well over average height, he is a man who can safely be imitated. His plane is not at either extreme, and he has probably given more thought to his swing than any other player.

At the beginning of his career, his swing was an aesthetic pleasure to observe – a loop at the top of a swing can give more impression of grace and rhythm than the more functional up-and-down movement. But Faldo wanted to build himself the mechanical perfection he felt would withstand the enormous pressure of contending over the last few holes of a major tournament. You could say that he thought his 'Mark One' swing was good enough to win tournaments, but not the ones which guarantee a kind of immortality.

The rest is history.

AT THE TOP

Let's assume that you have started back correctly, that you have remained in the correct plane, and that you have completed your swing away from the ball. Let's stop you there, for a moment, and examine the features which should be present once you have got the clubhead into, what the pro's call, 'the slot', and you are about to swing down to the ball.

(1) If your grip is a good one, the face of your club should be parallel to the target line – not open or closed to it.

(2) Your shoulders should be turned as much as your own flexibility allows. Some can't quite achieve a complete right-angle, others manage a little more. Failing to complete that shoulder turn is one of golf's most common faults, partly because many golfers are too hand-conscious. They get the club up there on high all right, but only by pushing upwards with the hands and lifting their arms in order to do so.

(3) The fullness of your swing determines where your toe points. Perhaps the ideal is 'at the ground', which happens when the length of your backswing positions the shaft

In the slot.

Checking angle of shaft and clubhead position.

Checking wrist-break.

Good position at the top.

A good shoulder turn.

Again, a good shoulder turn.

parallel to the ground. As I say, this is ideal, but many players have played golf superbly with a much shorter swing: remember Doug Sanders, who, they used to quip, 'could swing in a phone box'?

Many others travel on past the horizontal. This is perfectly acceptable, and perhaps even beneficial, because the player then has more time and space to develop clubhead speed in a relatively leisurely way.

But extra length can be achieved, even with a swing fault. Players can allow the clubhead to drop when they have reached the effective end of the backswing, probably in an attempt to achieve the maximum distance from the ball. Dropping the clubhead in this way, however, achieves nothing, and provides less control over the club.

(4) Hand position. It's possible to make a full shoulder turn, but still end up with the hands only a little above shoulder height at the end of the backswing. This isn't a disaster, but it does result in a shorter swing arc. If you become conscious of stretching away from the ball, then this certainly involves the arms, giving width to the swing, and placing the hands naturally well above shoulder height. Remember, though, this must be as the result of a swing, and not a lift.

ABOVE LEFT AND RIGHT: Has the clubhead been allowed to drop?

Low hands.

High hands.

Back to something like the address position before the hands come in.

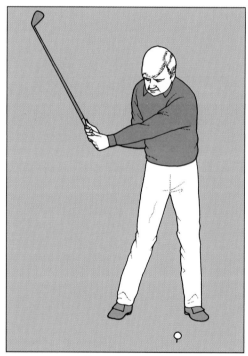

Body returns to address position before hands and arms.

BACK TO THE BALL

The first few inches of the backswing are the most vital moments of a golf swing, but even when this and all the rest of the backswing are performed to perfection, disaster can still follow. Your backswing only sets you up with the best chance of carrying out the downswing successfully.

So let's start with some 'don'ts'.

(1) As we've seen, some golfers are much too 'hand-conscious'. For them, it's quite natural to throw the hands at the ball as the main movement of the downswing. This may be effective in a game such as table tennis, where there's relatively little body movement in making a shot, but it doesn't work for golf.

(2) The shoulders contain some of the most powerful muscles in the body, so it seems natural, to some people, to try to make the most of them. They do this by heaving their shoulders at the ball, in an attempt to gain clubhead speed, but succeed only in getting themselves out of plane. The usual result is a clubhead path across the target line, producing a slice or a pull hook.

(3) Swinging back at the ball with the feeling that it's your arms which really count is a lesser disaster than the two previous faults. You might even manage to play passable golf with this swing, while letting the lower body take care of itself. But you won't play *good* golf.

The downswing must be led by the lower body – hips, legs, and let's not forget the feet. Golfers tend to hold key thoughts about how to initiate the journey back to the ball, some, for example, 'kicking off' with the right foot. Others think of turning the hips back towards the ball, and a few concentrate on beginning to straighten the left leg. That's all very well, but such a thought must not be taken in isolation. Feet, legs and hips make another of those one-piece movements, working rhythmically and in unison.

These parts of the anatomy should have returned to something like their position at the address, even before the hands and arms come into play at all, and during the time it takes the shoulders to make about half a turn.

This lower-body movement is common to all good players. You'll never see a competent golfer with a poor leg action, or an incompetent player with a good one. The poor player is far too preoccupied with thoughts about their hands, or about heaving with their shoulders: the legs are ignored and a very badly balanced and ineffective swing is the result. So, I repeat, the lower body must lead the downswing, and is the basis of a golf swing.

Meanwhile, what *has* happened to the hands and arms?

They should have remained passive, but that lower-body

TOP LEFT AND RIGHT AND ABOVE: Good and relaxed leg action, different viewpoints.

Clubhead and hands at impact, increasing the loft of an iron with the ball forward in the stance.

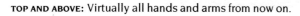

TOP AND ABOVE: Virtually all hands and arms from now on.

movement back to the ball does have an effect, namely to pull the arms down to approximately hip level. By themselves, the arms do nothing at all.

But their moment is coming! The rest of the down and through swing is virtually all hands and arms, and they provide by far the greatest part of clubhead speed.

Even at this late point in the swing, even when everything has gone very well indeed, your action can still go fatally wrong. And the crucial point is the position of the left wrist at impact.

So many poor players produce a flicking movement in that final moment. When they meet the ball, the left wrist is already flexed, forcing the palm of the hand to face the floor.

The left wrist should remain firm, with the back of the hand facing the target, and the palm facing to the rear, just as it does in the address position. Let's think of what happens if it does flex in the impact area of your swing.

You can try it out for yourself in slow motion. Two things are immediately apparent.

If you are using an iron, the blade will rapidly increase in loft, and just as certainly, it will become more open. All golfers who allow the wrists to flex too early are habitual slicers – unless they grip the club in an extremely shut position – and, usually, they will hit the ball very high, because they have turned the loft of a 5-iron into, say, a 7-iron.

From time to time, such golfers will play quite good golf, and on a good day, their timing of the wrist-break will be fairly consistent. But the slice and loss of distance will surely still be there. 'All right,' you may say, 'that can be compensated by using straight-faced irons, more so than should be needed for a shot of that length. So it doesn't matter in the least.'

Quite so. But you won't be in the least pleased about your loss of distance with driver and fairway woods.

Far more important, how can you hope to meet the ball with the same amount of wrist break each time? No. That firm left wrist is the recipe for consistency. Let the lesson be – the left wrist must still be in the address position at impact.

The left wrist flexed too early.

This is how it should be. Left arms and club still in a straight line.

An elevated tee.

TOP AND ABOVE: Shoulders move through about 90 degrees.

A poor turn.

Heaving with the shoulders.

THE SHOULDERS

There is nothing at all complicated about the correct movement of the shoulders. They turn from a position parallel with the target line at address, through 90 degrees, or more, at the top of the backswing, and back to the address position at impact.

This is easier said than done. In the heat of competition, you'll often hear a pro bemoan 'I didn't make a good turn', meaning that he didn't complete a full shoulder turn so that he got his back to the target. This will almost certainly have meant that his shoulders were open when he got back to the ball. Instead they should have been, once more, parallel to the target line.

The poor golfer's problems, however, are far worse. The shoulders, too, make that incomplete turn, and almost every time, the power is seen as coming from the upper body. They lash too early with their hands, heave with their shoulders, and find themselves far too open at the moment of impact. The swing path is disastrously across the ball, right to left, and the result is a slice, often quite severe, if the clubface is square or open at impact, and a fairly sharp left pull if it is closed.

SOURCES OF CLUBHEAD SPEED

I suggest that, at this point, you dissect your swing, bit by bit, with all the movements carried out correctly. Try the lower body – feet, legs, hips – first. There doesn't seem to be much speed from that area, does there?

Now the shoulders and back. A little more? But not much. So far, you have seen all those powerful thigh, back and shoulder muscles provide very little in the way of clubhead speed, though, admittedly, they do help. In the main, as I have already stressed, they provide the mechanical basis so that the hands and arms can lash the clubhead through the target line. They are vital in moving heavy weights – but a golf club isn't exactly heavy.

Primarily, to hit a long ball, what is needed is the ability to accelerate a light weight – a golf clubhead and shaft. And that's done by a combination of hand and arm speed.

CLOCKWISE: Complete swing sequence.

TEE SHOTS

For most club golfers, the aim is to hit the ball as far as possible. There are few who don't boast, on return to the clubhouse, that 'I reached the 320-yard 14th off the tee today!' Or 'Dammit, if I didn't put my tee shot into that stream across the 12th. Must be all of 300 yards!'

Yet there is little doubt that Greg Norman let in Mark Calcavecchia to win the 1989 British Open at Royal Troon simply by driving the ball too far.

You have to decide if these bunkers are in range.

Could you drive straight between the avenue of trees in the distance? Better to play short of them with an iron.

There is very little room for error on this tee. An accurate drive is needed between the trees, which are waiting for those wayward shots.

On the last hole of the four-hole play-off, Norman unleashed one of his thunderbolts and reached a bunker that everyone had found to be out of range all week. With that shot went the Championship, yet Greg had been warned that he might reach it if the adrenalin was in full flow. It was Jack Nicklaus who had said so, and he was proved right. If Norman had played a 3-wood he might well have become Champion for the second time.

So, unless your priority is telling a good tale in the clubhouse, rather than arriving there with a good score under your belt, the purpose of the tee shot is not to hit far enough to reach a bunker or a water hazard.

'But,' you could argue 'there aren't many lay-up tee shots on an average golf course.' That's true. Apart from sand, such hazards as water, belts of rough, or the occasional quarry, are much more likely to be intended to threaten a second shot. Only the exceptionally long drivers are menaced by them.

So we all want to hit the tee shot as far as we can, but that distance can still be a disadvantage, and I don't mean just because we might reach trouble.

Before playing your tee shot, you should always think first about where the green is. Then go further. Can you see the day's flag position? If you know the course well, where do you want to hit and stop on the green? Perhaps to give yourself an uphill putt?

ABOVE AND RIGHT: If your tee shot reaches here,
you'll have to take a penalty drop.

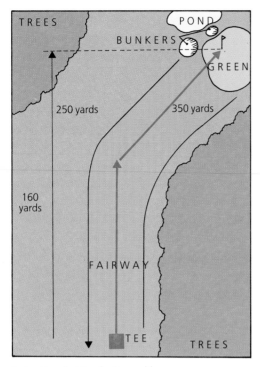

A short tee shot to a better position.

From the right of this fairway you wouldn't have to try to draw your second shot around the trees.

When you've analysed these matters, it will become obvious that the shot to the green (or the second shot on a par 5) isn't always best played from the centre of the fairway, however long your tee shot. If, for example, the green slopes only a little from right to left, you'll have a far better chance of stopping your ball predictably if you are coming in from the left, because of the increased bite you'll get when pitching into an upslope, however slight.

On the other hand, if the flag is set on the extreme left of the green, you may need to change your thinking. Coming in from the left will give you no room to work in, and from this angle, you'll have to pitch short, possibly catch up in some rough. In that case, your ball will not behave quite as predictably as if you can land directly on the green. So, you'll decide to discount the downslope (there will be plenty of green to play with when the flag is on the left), and play your tee shot down the right of the fairway.

If you are on the left of this fairway, you have to play for the flag over water.

The main problem here is out of bounds along the left.

You wouldn't want to play to this flag from well left.

But you haven't finished thinking yet. Next, you will need to consider the immediate surrounds of the green. Are there any bunkers, or other hazards? Almost certainly there are. And remember, such threats to your score aren't just sand and water. You'll obviously be looking out for potentially hazardous trees and bushes, but also note whether the ground falls away sharply, either to left or right of the green. If it does, then a chip or short pitch will be much less likely to finish close to the hole. Generally speaking, it is sensible to come in from the side which presents fewest problems between you and the flag.

Only after you have analysed these, and any other, problems should you consider playing your tee shot. A 160-yard tee shot down the right, for example, could leave you with a better line in to the flag than a 250-yard drive along the left.

Remember the golden rule: A good drive sets you up to play the rest of the hole. Viewed in isolation, it's worth very little, apart from the exhilaration that comes with hitting long and high.

PROBLEMS FROM THE TEE

So far we have looked at problems, in the area of the green, which need to be considered before a tee shot is played. However, many golfers don't get that far in their thinking, being far more concerned with immediate problems – those directly facing the tee shot.

LEFT: Keep your eye on the ball when there's water in front of the tee.

With the sea to the left, and gorse on the right,
you've got to aim accurately.

With dangers like this on either side you must
hit the fairway with your tee shot. It will cost you
dearly if you don't.

Arnold Palmer watches Christy O'Connor drive off.

The one which most concerns every golfer, at any level, is the presence of trouble either side of the fairway. Let's imagine that we are playing a hole with water on the left, and out of bounds' on the right. Just to make things more interesting, let's also suppose that the fairway is humpbacked, like the 10th on the Open Championship course at Turnberry. In fact, let's imagine that a drive which is only a fraction off dead centre will run you towards trouble, particularly when the ground is hard, whether you err from left to right.

Doesn't worry you in the least? Driving well today? Fine. By all means, blaze away. But if doubts do creep in, don't let them cramp your swing. Remember that the backswing must always be completed. You'll find that the ball tends to go straighter when you swing full out: don't be tempted to hold something in reserve in the vain hope of gaining greater control. That *never* works.

Let's now be a little more realistic, even if slightly more pessimistic. Let's say you haven't been driving badly, but aren't completely confident of getting a really straight one away.

Immediately, you should be thinking in terms of leaving the driver in the bag – which doesn't mean automatically reaching for the 3-wood. Many club golfers never even

Checking alignment to aim away from out of bounds along the right.

Hitting left.

consider hitting an iron to the fairway, but the pros think very differently.

What will the safe shot be on our imaginary terror hole? Basically, the only way to hold this fairway is to hit one of the upslopes with either a slight fade or draw. You should be thinking 5-iron, denying yourself the pleasure this time of the long, straight drive, realizing that it is all too likely to cost you strokes.

Let's now cut our tee shot problems by 50%, removing our imaginary 'out of bounds' area on the right, but retaining the water on the left. When your confidence is peaking, you can probably ignore it. When it isn't, take up your stance on the left of the teeing area, and play away from the trouble. By doing this you've given yourself a 45-degree margin of error, and even quite a sizeable hook probably won't find the water. Teeing up on the left in this way makes the big difference, and gives you a much better chance of avoiding trouble than simply aiming down the right of the fairway.

TOP, CENTRE AND ABOVE: If you're confident enough that you can draw the ball, you can aim at the out of bounds and watch your ball drift back again.

ABOVE: You have to aim right of centre to cope with this sloping fairway when the ground is hard.

DRIVING TO A DOGLEG

When playing a dogleg par 4, you'll often have the option of carrying the angle. You need to consider what length of carry is required, and how severely you'll be punished if you fail. Success, however, will often mean a relatively short pitch to the green and a birdie opportunity. For long hitters, the reward for carrying a dogleg is a chance of reaching the green in one.

If you decide that you can't make the carry, or that the risks are too great, then you should be thinking of the right placement for your tee shot. The degree of accuracy required rules out the driver, and indeed it's often all too possible to run out of fairway and finish in the rough.

As before, consider greenside problems and flat position, and set yourself up to reach the best second shot you can.

THE BEST SHAPE OF SHOT

Most professionals aim to drive with fade or draw, calculating that one consistent pattern gives them more fairway to work with. The fader, for example, can aim a little into the rough on the left. Always providing the fade 'takes', they then have a large margin for error before running into trouble on their right, when the fade becomes an outright slice.

The fade has one great advantage for players ranging from the great to the merely competent. Fade spin is greater than draw spin, and increases the chances of holding the fairway. Even quite ordinary players don't seem to have days which are quite as bad as those who draw the ball. Many pro's who prefer consistency to absolute length quite deliberately settle on this type of shot: Jack Nicklaus, Nick Faldo and Ben Hogan (who wasn't a great player until he defeated his hook) are among the champions who favour this method.

However, there does seem to be a tendency, these days, for professionals to favour the draw. Extra length is a formidable advantage for consistent players. The very long driver can find themselves playing mid-irons into par 5's and, in still air, even quite long par 4's can be covered with a drive and a pitch. Your big driver is obviously far more likely to place those kinds of shot close to the flag than the golfer who is hitting woods or long irons from much greater distances.

This was the approach of the young Jack Nicklaus. Jack, himself, wrote that his method was to power it away with his seige-gun driving and then 'slop it on the green'.

Many of today's players would approve, although they wouldn't necessarily use the word 'slop'. They know perfectly

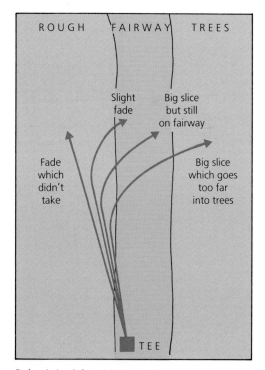

Driving at a short dogleg of 350 yards.

Fade, aiming left and drifting right.

The 'rough' comes in all different forms and this is one of the worst. The clubhead gets entangled with the grass and weeds on both the takeaway and again at the moment of impact.

well that the long tee shot is far more likely to finish off the fairway, but today's improved equipment combines with fast hand action to hold the green from poor lies in the rough.

For club players, the draw shape is likely to lead to problems. When you're not quite on top form, that little tail away to the left when the ball is well on its way stops behaving itself, and every tee shot becomes a quick hook. Extra distance is replaced by acute embarrassment.

Neither is the average club player very effective from the rough. Playing far less often than the pro, they haven't acquired anything like the wrist strength (I recall Peter Alliss telling me how much smaller his wrists became when he gave up tournament golf), and cannot get the clubhead through the rough and also retain control.

Overall, I must still come down on the side of the fade, but it is worth emphasising that a fade isn't a slice. The slice immediately starts going right, and continues in a parabola. The fade spends most of its time straight, and only moves left to right late in flight.

DRIVING IN WIND

TAIL WINDS

Let's assume you want maximum distance. Hitting the ball low will do little actual harm, but your ball will be flying below the full strength of the wind, and will not get maximum benefit from it. You therefore need to get the ball up into the air, and let the wind work on it. If you naturally hit a high ball, then all well and good. If not, you might start thinking in terms of the greater loft of a fairway wood.

HEADWINDS

Driving into the wind is a far more difficult proposition. The first thing to do is to avoid fighting it. It is very tempting to think that the wind is going to take 80 yards off your drive so that you must hit it harder, but that approach is fraught with danger.

For a start, this will destroy your rhythm, just at the time when the wind has already adversely affected your balance.

A persimmon head driver.

Ball on a high tee.

And also forward in the stance.

Even if you do bring it off, you'll still achieve precisely nothing.

That drive which would have travelled a delightful distance in still air will have been very well struck with high swing speed and will therefore have more backspin, as does any well-struck shot. Consequently, a harder drive won't give you increased distance, but greater backspin, causing your ball to soar upwards into the wind. Certainly, it will have travelled a great distance when it eventually comes back to earth, but most of that additional length will be up and down, rather than forward.

Obviously, the ball has to be kept low. There are several ways of doing this, including the one used by Seve Ballesteros and other tournament pro's.

In this method, the ball is teed up higher than usual, accepting the risk of getting under the ball, causing it to fly directly upwards off the top of the clubface. The ball is also placed a little further forward in the stance than is the norm. The aim is then to make contact on the upswing, the idea being to hit up at the ball, thereby reducing backspin and thus preventing the ball flying upwards as far as it might have done if it had been teed at normal height.

A low tee and the ball back in the stance.

Normal height of tee and ball position.

Another approach is quite the reverse. The ball is moved back a couple of inches in the stance and a low tee is used. The club is gripped a little lower, by a couple of inches, and the idea is to hold a mental image of the hands well ahead of the clubhead, which is pulled through the ball. If you try this, don't hit full out, and keep the wrists relatively inactive. Aim for a precise stroke, rather than a hard one.

SIDE WINDS

Again, there are two very different ways of approaching this problem. One is to play your normal shot, but allow for the effect of the wind. Then simply allow 10, 20 or even 50 yards of drift, according to wind speed. Also remember that a side wind reduces your distance, although the major effect is on your direction.

This is the easiest way to counter a side wind, but players with the skill to shape their shots either way can handle the problem differently. In a left-to-right wind, play a draw and, when the wind is coming into your body, play a fade. Shape of shot and wind effects then cancel each other out. The professionals call it 'holding the ball into the wind'.

A poor tee shot can land you in all sorts of trouble.

HITTING IRONS TO THE FAIRWAY

One of the biggest thrills in golf is hitting the ball a very long way. But an even bigger one is a good score. And that means thinking as well as hitting.

When playing a tight course many professionals make little use of the driver, often only using it when they really do need the distance, say, on the par 5's and long par 4's. Otherwise their thinking is that it's much better to play the next shot from the fairway than from the trees, or after taking a penalty drop from the water.

Here's where the 1-iron comes into play. It's a difficult club, except in skilled hands, however, and many club golfers don't feel confident until they have something with the loft of a 4- or 5-iron in their hands. If that's your feeling, then use a more lofted iron. After all, the idea is to play a safe shot to the fairway, so there's no sense in taking a longer iron – you might even be more effective with your normal driver.

I know – you lose the pleasure of a long drive, but there's a different sort of enjoyment in placing your tee shot precisely, and knowing that you've used brain instead of brawn.

Irons also come into play when you're not sure whether you might reach trouble – sand, water, rough – with your driver. If you know you can't carry a hazard but fear you might reach it, then the obvious decision is to play short.

ABOVE LEFT AND RIGHT: Taking an iron from the tee.

Why not lay up short of the water, rather than risk a difficult carry?

FAIRWAY WOODS FROM THE TEE

If you have a favourite 3- or 4-wood, one with which you are confident you can play safe, you could often use it as an alternative to an iron from the tee. Indeed, as there is little loss of distance involved, a wood with some loft might lower your score, if played throughout your round.

During the 1990 British Open at St Andrews, Nick Faldo often chose a 2-wood, and such past champions as Peter Thomson and Bobby Locke often didn't even carry a driver, in the interests of keeping on the fairway.

HOW TO DRAW AND FADE

In this section, I'm going to assume that the basic shape of your shot is straight. If you are, for example, an habitual slicer, don't think that you can cure your fault by tacking this

The Trevino set-up.

An open clubface at address is likely to produce a slice instead of a fade.

A slightly closed clubface will probably cause the hook as opposed to the intended draw.

or that draw technique on to a fundamentally poor grip, swing plane or stance.

The general technique of Lee Trevino points some lessons. He has won six majors – US Open and British Open twice each, and a couple of PGA Championships, as well as a whole host of other tournaments. Now entering his fifties he still remains a major force and number one on the Seniors Tour.

The young Trevino hooked the ball, but having watched Ben Hogan, another natural hooker, decided that the fade was the pattern of shot for him. One of Hogan's basic recipes was to move his left hand slightly anti-clockwise. Trevino, however, didn't wish to change his grip, which features the so-called 'strong' left-hand grip, with perhaps three knuckles showing. Although his right-hand grip is more conventional, with the 'V' pointing towards his right shoulder, it is still much stronger than used by most pro's today. This means that, at the top of his swing, his clubface is very shut – at right angles to the target – rather than parallel with it. For most of us, if the swing were normal, this ought to produce a pull or hook, or both together!

To fade the ball, Trevino does various things. In the first place, he stands at an angle of about 45 degrees open to his target line. If you saw a player with this kind of stance on your

TOP LEFT AND RIGHT, AND ABOVE: Open, square and closed with an iron.

club's practice ground, you'd dismiss them as hopeless.

He also stands with his ball, apparently, too far forward – just about opposite his left toe. These two positions would guarantee a slice for most of us, but Trevino's shut clubface makes all the difference.

Now we come to the swing back to the ball. Trevino leads strongly with his legs, slides his hips along the target line, and keeps his hands dead. His attack on the ball is almost entirely a pull, coming from the left side of his body, and continuing after impact. The result is a swing across the ball and a clubface which is still square on: only if he wants to draw the ball does Trevino let his hands into the action, closing the face a little at impact.

There could be hints here for the club golfer, but the total method would surely be disastrous. It only works for Lee Trevino because other movements in his swing are so extreme that they make it relatively easy for him to detect which part of his swing mechanism has gone wrong.

By comparison, the Jack Nicklaus system for fading and drawing the ball is simplicity itself. He goes for complete orthodoxy, hitting a straight shot and making just one adjustment. He sets his club in his grip so that the blade is slightly open for the fade or closed for the draw – and, obviously enough, he also adjusts his aim to allow for drift.

To the Nicklaus method for the fade we can add other touches:

(1) Like Trevino, set your ball further forward in your stance.

(2) Again, like Trevino, open your stance.

(3) Weaken your left-hand grip, but be wary of the fact that changing your grip can feel uncomfortable. Nicklaus maintains the same grip, adjusting only the club.

(4) Keep the hands quiet, using a pulling movement through the ball.

To obtain draw, simply do the reverse, although there is perhaps one exception. Closing the stance isn't advisable for most people, probably giving the feeling that your left side is in the way and inhibiting the full swing.

USES OF DRAW AND FADE FROM THE TEE

(1) If a fairway slopes strongly, especially if that slope is towards a hazard, a shot drifting in the opposite direction should help you hold the fairway, even when the ground is hard.

(2) The shape of a hole usually means that a shot of the same shape is very useful. Let's consider a par 4, swinging gently from right to left, but not a sharply angled dogleg. A straight tee shot will do well enough, but a draw will follow the fairway

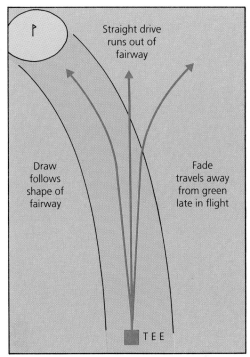

Following the shape of a fairway.

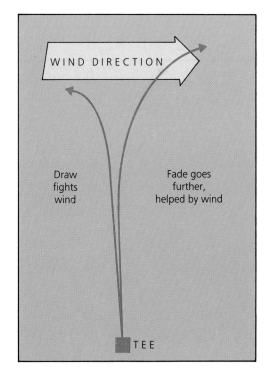

Draw and fade in left to right wind.

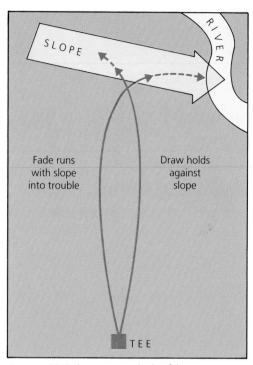

Draw and fade from tee to a sloping fairway.

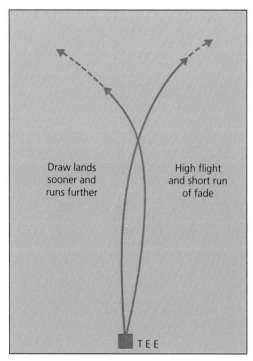

Flight and run of draw and fade.

curve, in effect, giving a longer drive. A fade, in these circumstances, will end by almost travelling away from the green, leading to a longer second shot.

(3) You can also use the wind for greater length. If, for example, you are driving with the wind blowing on your back (left to right), a fade will be helped along, while a draw would be fighting the wind. However, this only applies in light to medium winds: trying to make use of a gale in this way is far too risky.

It is just as likely that your ball will be swept away, so it is better to use draw or fade to combat a strong wind, obtaining a more controlled tee shot.

(4) The fade gives a relatively high tee shot, the draw a lower one. The fade stops relatively quickly on landing, the draw lands more quickly and is likely to run. You can therefore use the draw for maximum length when the ground is firm or hard, and the fade to a soft fairway. In the second case, there would be little run, and a fade carries further through the air.

PRACTISING YOUR DRIVING

I always think that the term 'driving range' is dangerous. It encourages golfers to take out a bucket of balls and hit them away, flat out. The phrase 'practice range' is preferable, implying that you can use all the clubs in the bag, and not just the driver.

Hitting at maximum power all the time can lead you off course, especially if you don't do that when you are out on the course. It can also destroy your rhythm.

So let's start with a general 'don't'. *Don't* stand there on a driving range or practice ground and simply hit out. Professionals always try to keep something in reserve, because precision and rhythm are far more important than the chance to occasionally hit an exceptionally long ball.

Here's what you should do:

■ *Avoid hitting at maximum power.*

Always try to keep balanced and rhythmic, and limit yourself to what feels like about 80% effort.

■ *Always select a target to aim at.*

Don't merely try out your full swing. Your tee shot will always be aimed at a small area of fairway, so reflect this in your practice.

■ *Vary the shape of your shot.*

Left-to-right, right-to-left, high and low. You won't, for example, be able to play a left-to-righter in the real life of the golf course by magic. You have to learn how to do these things in practice.

■ *Learn the distance you hit the ball.*

Ignore short mis-hits and long balls alike. The good

The player will want to avoid bunkers, the humpy ground right and left and also be along the left side of the fairway for the best line to the flag.

Don't just use the driver from the tee.

average is what you should have in mind. Your driving is good when that length is consistent, so that there is only about 20 yards between your longest and shortest balls.

▨ *Don't practise only driving, just before a serious round.*

This is when you should be concentrating on warming up, and on touch and rhythm. Just hitting with the driver alone won't help your game.

▨ *Only practise with driver alone when that club is giving you trouble.*

Most practice sessions are more valuable using all, or most, of the clubs in your bag. If it *is* to be the driver, don't practise too long. The energy you exert can rapidly tire you. At least pause for rest and thought between shots, and always think about what you are aiming to achieve with each one. Swishing ball after ball away without pause may be good exercise, but it isn't golf.

But perhaps there is one exception. Jimmy Demaraet once watched Ben Hogan playing a very, very long session of 3-woods. To Demaraet they all seemed to be excellent shots, so he approached Hogan and asked Hogan what he was seeking to achieve. Said Hogan:

'I'm trying to see how I play the club when I'm tired.'

EQUIPMENT

I n theory, any club can be used for a tee shot and in practice, nearly all of them are used from time to time. Only the putter can be said to be a total exception, even though you are allowed to use one.

In this book, however, I will deal only with some thoughts on choosing a driver. The other clubs are referred to elsewhere in the *Golf Instructor's Library*.

CHOOSING A DRIVER

Let there be no mistake about it. The driver is one of the most vital clubs to get right. Forget that tired old saying, 'You drive for show and putt for dough.' I know that there's a valid point being made. A 300 yard drive down the middle soon becomes unimportant if followed by a volley of poor shots and a three putt.

I say forget the phrase because a good tee shot enables you to play the rest of the hole. The brilliance of your putting will be worthless if you've previously hit three driver shots in a row out of bounds.

There are various tales of star golfers who have stayed faithful to the same driver for many years, perhaps even their whole career. Sam Snead is one example.

Immediately he appeared on the US Tour, he was successful and quickly recognized as a potentially great player, perhaps one already. But Sam knew he was likely to snap hooks his drives from time to time. Wild tee shots mean that a professional can't compete, except on good days. He wants to be sure that he can hit most of the fairways and that a really wild teeshot is going to be a rare occurrence, even when playing well below form.

Sam quickly found the answer when given quite a heavy club by Henry Picard. The extra weight, Sam thinks, helped him control his swing. He played with it for year upon year. It

Choosing the right equipment is as important as choosing the right line off the tee.

Drivers come in different sizes and weights. Furthermore the heads can
be made from metal, laminated maple or persimmon. But the important
thing, when buying one, is to make sure you feel comfortable with it.

was repaired again and again. Eventually, it was very likely a
substantially different club to swing than it had been
originally. But to Snead it was the same club. It gave him
confidence.

That's what you want most of all in a driver. There's no
easy way to find either the right club or confidence but, once
you have it, be like Snead and, even if you don't always use
the club, keep it by you.

A variety of factors will make up your ideal driver. As for
Sam Snead, weight is as important as anything. For every
golfer there is an ideal. No one can quite predict what it will
be. Thinking of length alone, this is the balance between
weight and clubhead speed. A heavier club swung at the same
speed as a lighter one will hit the ball further. The lighter club
will propel the ball further, however, if that lighter weight
means you can accelerate the clubhead at higher velocity.

Accuracy with the club is an entirely different matter.
Snead found that a heavier club helped him control his swing.
Others, however, using a heavy club might become wild off
the tee in their endeavours to accelerate a weight that is too
much for them.

The answer, of course, is that experimenting is
necessary. Try out used clubs, borrow others. Perhaps your
club professional will even tape new ones to avoid their being
marked. If you've the money, you can buy new ones from time

to time and part exchange them if they prove not to fit your swing.

As regards accuracy, the loft of the clubface is very important. A driver with an 8 degree loft will enable most players to get a longer tee shot than with a 12 degree loft. But the straighter-faced club is far less forgiving to a less than perfect strike. Most will find the 12 degree loft gives a more consistent result.

Length, but not accuracy and consistency, can also come, at least in part, from the materials used in the construction of the club.

Let's take the head first. Not so many years ago, there wasn't much choice. It was either solid persimmon or laminated wood. Many would say that in practice there wasn't much difference. Persimmon gave more delight to the eye but was more likely to crack than a laminated head. Greater or lesser distance was probably more a matter of the golfer's feelings about the club than any actual mechanical difference. Anyway, it was an insert that was brought into contact with the ball, not wood at all.

This brings us to the secret of the widespread acceptance of metal drivers. Do they cause the ball to leave the clubface with greater velocity? Many have found this to be

Plenty of room on the right, but watch the out of bounds on the left.

A light-weight steel shafted wood. The red laminated insert is there to assist in lining up the clubhead with the ball at address.

the case. If all other factors are equal, why should this be so? The answer has to be the harder material used.

Shafts are even more important. As regards length, the lightness of the shaft governs the weight that can be put into the head. The ideal is impossible – a shaft that weighs nothing at all. However, much work has gone into developing lighter shafts that still retain strength, but without increasing any tendency for them to twist while retaining desirable flex characteristics.

The first developments, after the triumph of the steel shaft over hickory, was in lighter weight steels, and since then all manner of materials have been used as a substitute for steel. Glass fibre, aluminium, titanium, carbon fibre and boron are a few examples.

How do average golfers decide? The answer is that they surely can't, but should seek professional advice and sound information. Discuss the matter with your club professional, who can analyse your swing and estimate, primarily, what weights and flex characteristics will suit you best. The old rule of thumb was that the stiff shaft ought to suit hard hitters while gentle swingers benefited from more flexible shafts. Hard hitters couldn't use flexible shafts because these flexed too much when swung fast. Gentle swingers felt they had a rigid pole in their hands when using a stiff shaft and lost the benefit of a 'kick' from a more flexible shaft. But there is more to it than that.

Where the club flexes is also important and has a strong influence on distance, accuracy and ball trajectory. The experienced eye of the club professional comes into play. They also have equipment which could help.

Even so, I feel it isn't an exact science and the golfer isn't a machine. In the end, it's not only the characteristics of the club but also how consistently the golfer reproduces his or her basic swing characteristics.

Provided the golf bag does its job it doesn't need to be as exotic as this one. However, if you can lay your hands on the clubs in this bag don't ever sell them, they're collectors' items.

CARE OF YOUR DRIVER AND WOODS

If your 'woods' are made of metal, the heads need virtually no attention. I could go further and say that their performance won't be affected in any measurable degree however scratched and nicked they become. But you do need to give the faces of these clubs a few seconds' attention, to clean out the mud and crushed grass forced into the grooves. They help put backspin on the ball, which helps with control. If you obtained no backspin at all, actually an impossibility because of the loft on all clubs, the ball would dip rather than climb.

Sometimes a casual wipe-over will be sufficient, but crushed grass can be surprisingly tenacious. If this proves to be so, any brush with stiff bristles will accomplish the task.

A normal nail brush can be used for cleaning out the grooves on your clubs. Avoid using scourers, they could damage the club face.

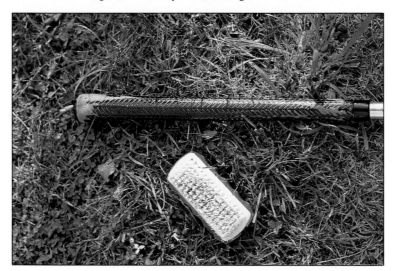

Again, a soft nail brush can be used for cleaning the grip on your club. However, scouring won't do any harm this time; in fact it will probably improve your hold on the grip.

A full-cord grip. The pattern is not there for decoration only, it is there to help you with the correct alignment of the clubhead at address.

A fine example of a golfer looking after his clubs and keeping them in good condition.

An example of a wooden-headed club with a brass sole insert. Few of these clubs are used these days.

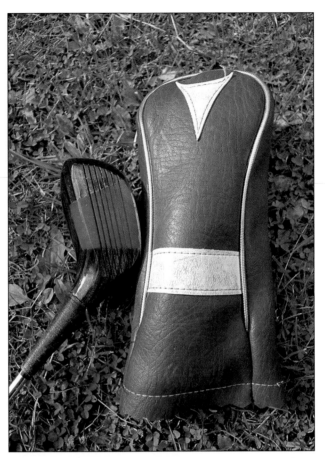

Take the head covers off to allow the clubs to dry naturally.

Woods that are actually made of wood can be cleaned in precisely the same way but the scratches and nicks are highly significant. They allow wet and damp to get through to the wood beneath the impermeable finish.

There are other areas to look out for on a wooden clubhead. The constant impact with ball and turf causes the finish to eventually crack around the face insert and the sole plate.

After playing in wet weather you should always allow the clubs to dry out naturally. Never leave head covers on. (These will often be wet as well, which means they make your clubheads wetter as well as preventing the air getting to them.) Of course the drying process will be speeded if you take the trouble to use a dry cloth on your heads.

However, these precautions don't solve the problem of damp getting into the clubs in the first place. There is only one solution. Examine them carefully from time to time and, when you notice any deterioration, have them re-finished in your professional's shop.

Modern shafts need no attention, though you may like to maintain their appearance, cosmetically speaking, by wiping them over with a damp cloth.

Grip condition is vital and I'm amazed how little attention the majority of golfers pay to them. In my opinion

The popular persimmon-headed driver, used by the majority of golfers.

The increasingly popular carbon fibre headed driver, which many of the top class players use these days

. . . but, don't pick the carbon fibre driver just because your favourite golfer uses one. You must always choose one that you feel happy with.

The value of head covers were appreciated in the early days of golf as this cover shows. Its design was basic but its purpose was the same as the cover of today.

most modern golf grips are contemptible. I suspect they are designed to wear out as quickly as possible. You should, alas, be prepared to have them replaced by your professional every six months. This is because they quickly lose their essential 'tackiness', which helps you hold on to the club securely, and soon become smooth.

There is something you can do to restore the tacky feel. Your hands are always greasy and sometimes sweaty and dirty as well. An invisible deposit forms on the grip. Remove it by scrubbing with a brush, some detergent and soap. Rinse very thoroughly or else you will be worse off than when you began the operation. Soap and detergent are slippery substances.

As the grips deteriorate, this simple treatment becomes less effective. I'm afraid, for the clubs used the most frequently, it will last only one round of golf.

The days before the mass production market; a pair of craftsman made woods.

The persimmon head can be found on most woods these days but this one, with the boron shaft, is gradually making its presence felt

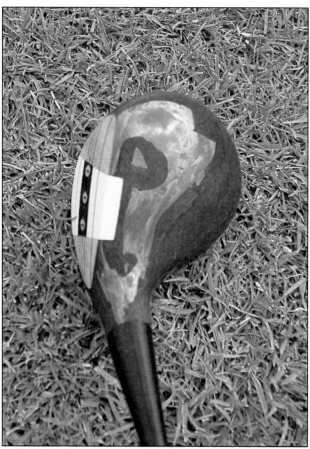

... however, the persimmon-headed wood with steel shaft remains the most popular wood amongst club golfers.

Another modern-day innovation is the ceramic headed 'wood'. Those shown here have the boron shafts.

Golf clubs don't have to be this expensive, but if you want the latest in golfing technology then you have to pay for it.

Choosing woods can be a hazardous task as this
vast selection in the pro's shop shows.

Despite the vast choice available, many
players still trust the laminated maple wood.

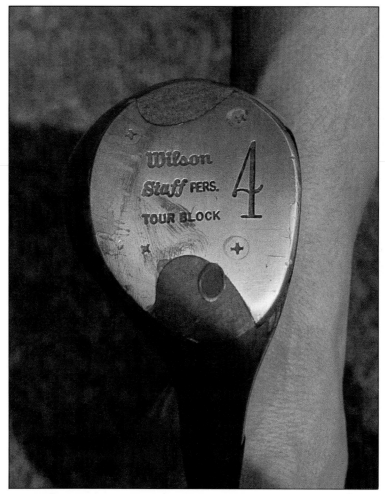

The sole plate of a modern-day club. Note how it differs from that shown on page 86. This is a No. 4 wood and is used for playing off the fairway.

But don't give up hope. There are alternatives, such as leather grips. They last for many years, but are relatively expensive and also need cleaning and refurbishing from time to time. I have recently discovered cord grips, probably the more practical of the alternatives. These grips are a little more expensive than standard ones and have a rough surface. I have not yet needed to clean mine and they give a very secure feeling, even in wet weather. But, like most things in life, nothing's perfect. They are a little harsh to delicate skin. Especially when practising, if your hold on the club allows any movement, chafing and even blistering will quickly result. However, this is a useful teaching aid. Your grip simply isn't good enough.

For a quick check, apply the Henry Cotton test. He told me, many years ago, that a golfer with a good grip should be able to line up six balls on the practice grounds and hit them all away without re-gripping. It was a very valid point. If you need to re-grip, you've allowed the club to slip in your grasp. This is an opportunity, like it or not, to examine the way you are holding the club. Whatever your grip, strong or weak, it must not allow the club to move in the hands.

The insert is the part of the wood that makes contact with the ball. Note
the screws on this insert; you should make sure they are flush with the
plate otherwise they will damage your ball and cause irregular flight
paths after contact.

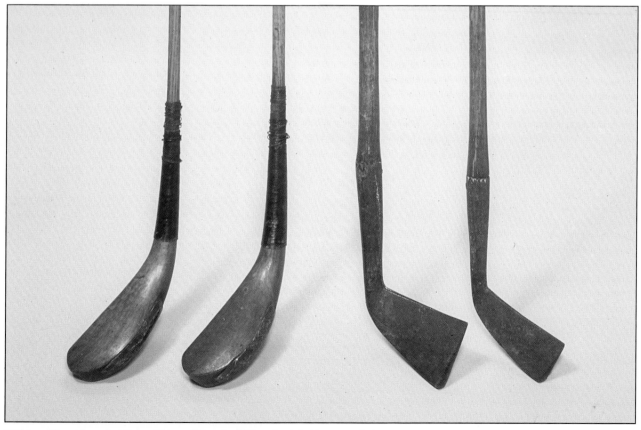

Eighteenth century woods and irons. If you look closely at the two woods
you will see that even in those days they had inserts on the faces.

GLOSSARY OF TECHNICAL TERMS USED

Address: standing to the ball, usually with the club grounded behind it.

Blade: the head of an iron club, sometimes including the putter when of similar shape to an iron.

Carrying the angle (of a dogleg)**:** hitting a ball, usually a tee shot, over a bend in the shape of the hole.

Chip: a shot played with an iron where most of the travel is along the ground rather than in the air.

Clearing the hips: the anti-clockwise movement of the hips which allows the through swing to take place.

Closed face: position of the club face in relation to the ball when the toe is slanted inwards; also the position of the clubhead at the top of the backswing when the club-face is square to the target line instead of the toe pointing along it.

Closed stance: when the left foot is closer to the target line than the right.

Dogleg: a shape of golf hole where, on a par 4 or par 5, the fairway bends sharply to a right-angle or almost so.

Draw: a shape of golf shot where the ball starts travelling to the right of target and then curves gently right to left.

Fade: a shape of golf shot where the ball starts by travelling to the left of target and then curves gently left to right.

Fairway woods: wooden (sometimes metal) clubs with more loft than a driver. The most commonly used are the 3 and 4, but many golfers use a 2-wood and a 5-wood.

Flat swing: a swing in which the golfer's hands, arms and club are not above shoulder level in the backswing.

Follow-through: the part of the golf swing which follows impact with the ball.

Good turn: when a golfer moves the shoulders 90 degrees or more on the backswing.

Green to play with: a golfer has little green to play with when playing to a hole close to the edge of the green nearest to them. There is plenty of green to play with when the hole is considerably further away.

Hazard: a bunker or marked area of water, stream, ditch or river.

Hooded face: the angle of a clubface when the golfer addresses or strikes the ball with the hands well ahead of the clubhead.

Hook: *see draw*, with the difference being the ball curves far more extremely right to left.

Impact: when clubhead strikes the ball.

Lateral head movement: when the head moves backwards, and perhaps forwards, during the golf swing.

Lay up: to play short (perhaps of some danger on the golf course).

Lie: how the ball is positioned on the ground.

Loft: the angle of a clubface.

Loop: a golf swing when the clubhead does not travel back and down on merely the same path, but loops round in the top part of the backswing.

Open face: position of the clubface in relation to the ball when the toe is slanted outwards; also the position of the clubhead at the top of the backswing, when the toe does not point along the target line but points away from the player to a greater or lesser extent.

Open shoulders: when the shoulders are not side on to the target, either at address position or as the player strikes the ball, but instead would show some, or a great deal, of chest to an observer standing in front of the player on the target line.

Open stance: when the left foot is withdrawn further from the ball than the right.

Out of bounds: land outside the golf course boundaries; sometimes areas inside the boundaries may be declared out of bounds – a practice ground is sometimes such an example.

Pitch: a high shot, anywhere between 10 and 150; yards, when the ball travels mostly through the air and with relatively little run; also the point where a golf ball lands on the ground.

Pull hook: a shot which goes to the left immediately from the clubface and then curves right to left.

Safe shot: playing in a direction or to a length which avoids some danger, either on the fairway or the green, when a bolder shot would present both danger and the prospect of greater reward.

Shaft: all the golf clubs other than the head. Most often made of tubular steel with other materials, such as carbon fibre, aluminium, glass fibre and wood.

Shut face: the position of the clubface in relation to the ball when the toe is slanted inwards; also the position of the clubhead at the top of the backswing when the toe of the club does not point along the target line but instead the clubface or clubhead is parallel with that line.

Slice: a shot where the ball immediately curves left to right from the clubface.

Slot: the position of the clubhead at the top of the backswing. Players aim to make this very consistent and may then say, 'I'm getting the club in the slot' or 'I can't get the club in the slot.'

Square face: when, at address, the clubface is parallel to an imaginary line drawn from ball to player.

Stance: position of the player as he or she stands to the ball, ready to swing.

Straight-faced iron: those irons with the least loft, usually irons 1 to 3.

Swing path: the route followed by the clubhead in backswing and downswing.

Target line: an imaginary line between ball and target.

Tee: an area of a golf course from which players begin playing a particular hole.

Tee peg: a small device, usually made of wood or plastic, on which golfers can place their ball before playing off from the teeing area.

Tee shot: a golf shot played from a teeing area.

Tee-up: to place a ball on a tee peg.

Upright swing: a swing where the player moves the club well above shoulder level, towards the head rather than the shoulder joint.

Vardon grip: a grip popularized by Harry Vardon around the end of the nineteenth century, where the notable feature is that the little finger of the right hand overlaps onto the forefinger of the left hand.

Waggle: movements of the clubhead after the player has addressed the ball but before beginning to swing back and play their shot.

Wrist-break: bending or flexing of the wrist joint.

INDEX